PAINTING FOR PEACE IN FERGUSON

CAROL SWARTOUT KLEIN

"When I was a boy and I would see scary things on the news, my mother would say to me, 'Look for the helpers. You will always find people who are helping.'"

Fred Rogers
The World According to Mister Rogers

Design Team: Robert O'Neil and Michael Kilfoy
Cover Calligraphy: Marie Enger
Photography: Michael Kilfoy, Ryan Archer, Rubin Roche, Carol Swartout Klein,
Jody Porter, Gussie Klorer, Dan Duncan, Kelley Ray and Robin Shively
Printing: Jaffe Book Solutions, St. Louis, MO

Printed in the United States. Library of Congress Control Number: 2015941032
ISBN: 978-0-9892079-9-7 Paperback
ISBN: 978-0-9963901-0-1 Hardback

Profits from the book will benefit youth and economic recovery programs in north St. Louis County. Additional tax deductible donations or gifts of books to area schools may be made to the Painting for Peace project through the Greater St. Louis Community Foundation.

For more information please visit
www.paintingforpeacebook.com

Dedicated to the people of Ferguson and St. Louis as they begin the steps of healing and creating a stronger and better community

In the small town of Ferguson
In 2014
Some people did things that
Were meaner than mean

Some people were mad
Some people were sad
But everyone, everywhere
Felt pretty bad ☹

Police were there
And protesters too
People were scared
Didn't know what to do

Some locked their doors
Boarded windows up tight
To help keep them safe
All through the long night

But when morning came
Folks took one look around
And said we don't like
The looks of our town

We have an idea
We know what to do
We'll bring out our paints
Red, Yellow and Blue

We'll **Paint** up those boards

That make us feel down

We'll paint pictures of LOVE

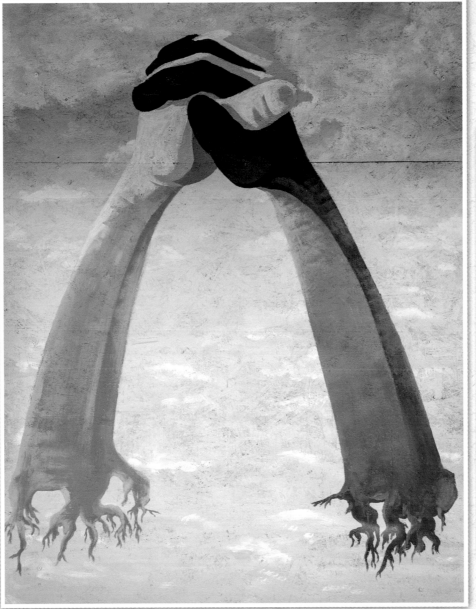

And bring **HOPE** to the town

13

14

And so they came out
On a day Sunny and Bright

Young folks **And** old folks

Black folks **And** white

COMING TOGETHER

WE ALL ♥ FERGUSON

CITY HALL

And down **South** near Shaw

With their **Paints** and their brushes

And started to Draw

They drew pictures of **Peace**

Of **Hope** and of **Light**

23

That show **Love's** even stronger

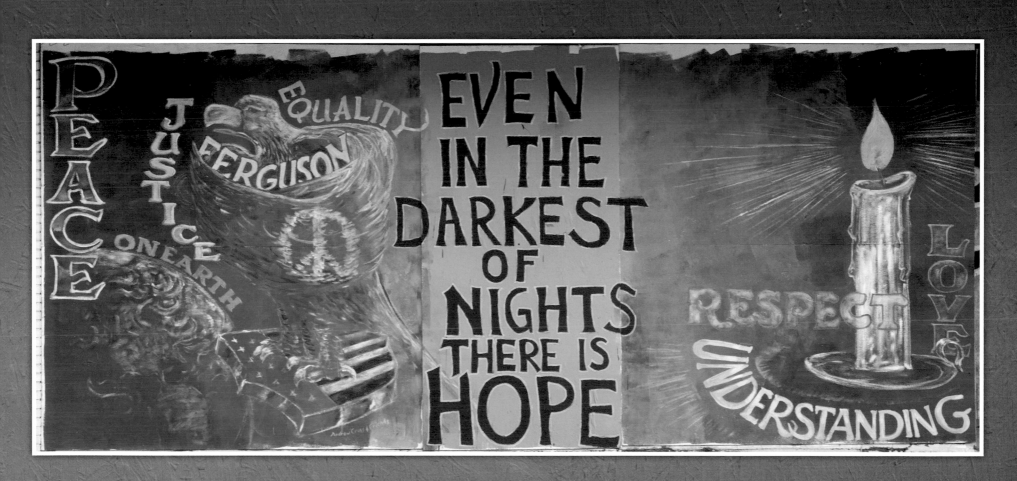

Than the **Darkest** of nights

UNLESS someone LIKE YOU cares a whole awful lot, nothing is going to get better, It's not. -The Lorax

SAVE OUR SONS

LOVE

HOPE

The Enemy Is Fear. We Think It Is Hate; But It Is Fear.

Gandhi

I refuse to accept the view that mankind is so tragically bound the starless midnight of racism and war that daybreak the of can I truth love bright peace never believe and will become have that a reality unarmed unconditional the final word -MLK Jr.

LOVE

JUSTICE

Some art had sayings

JUSTICE IS WHAT LOVE LOOKS LIKE IN PUBLIC

THEY THOUGHT THEY COULD BURY US...

THEY DIDN'T KNOW

WE WERE SEEDS

CENTER of Hope and Peace

STILL WE RISE

With **Words** that have power

Other art was from **Nature**

Long Live the Rose that that grew from the Concrete When no one else even cared...,..

A **Tree,** **Bird** or **Flower**

Some Dazzled with Colors

30

That Danced in the light

Other art was more Bold

By Kaite D. "think of all the still left around you and be happy"

Choose Love

STORM UP

PRAY FOR OUR CITY!/WORLD! ONE LOVE! it's the answer! Shine Your Light

#callme.r.r.artworks

309

Using just **Black** and *White*

As they **looked** down the street

They were **Proud** of their art

'Cause for things to get better

We must **Each** do our part

As we work Side by Side

And LOVE ONE another

Both **IN** and **OUT**-side

The Work is not finished

There's much more
to be done

PEACE LOVE IMO's

LETS HEAL

I HAVE DECIDED TO Stick WITH LOVE HATE IS TOO GREAT A BURDEN TO BEAR. ~MLK JR

But this Art

SNAPPY'S

ONE LOVE

I ♥ Ferg

HEAL

Power of Forgiveness

Children are our greatest treasure. — Nelson Mandela

We are OPEN

Shows the Spirit

PEACE StL

All we Need is Love

LOVE
PEACE
STL Together

WE WILL RISE
PEACE
IT'S IN OUR HANDS
Ferguson

United We Stand. DIVIDED WE FALL

"Great Leaders define Reality and give HOPE."
Peace Love

PEACE & LOVE

FERGUSON STRONG

UNITED WE STAND

INJUSTICE ANYWHERE IS A
THREAT TO JUSTICE *everywhere*

HOPE FOR EVERYONE

Help one another
for we are all in the same boat

PEACE

"A JOURNEY OF A
THOUSAND MILES
BEGINS WITH A
SINGLE STEP."
—LAO TZU

WORK
TOGETHER!
OPEN
come
in!

Show
me
LOVE

Believe There Is Good In The World

Be the CHANGE

STRENGTH

OPEN

SHALOM

UNITY

Of a new Ferguson

A Special Thanks to the following who made the citywide Paint for Peace effort a reality

Gail Babcock

Natasha Bahrami

Chris Bellers

Martin Casas

Jenny Churchill

Alderman Steve Conway

Laura Coppinger

Dana Sebastian-Duncan

Catherine Gilbert

Alderwoman Megan Green

Tom Halaska, Jr.

Dwane Ingram

Alderwoman Christine Ingrassia

Dwayne James

Gussie Klorer

Jen Kubiszewski

Mike and Lizzie Lonero

Bob McGartland

Jeff and Carey Morgan

Maria Price

Christopher Shearman

Gina Walsh

Rachel Witt

ArtBar

ArtMart

Cafe Natasha

Dick Blick Art Materials

The Ferguson Response

Ferguson Youth Initiative

Grand Center Arts Academy

Paint for Peace

Vincenzo's Restaurant

Thanks to the Artists and Volunteers who were a part of Painting For Peace

Rachel Abbinanti

Rosie Abramczyk

Phil & Gail Aho

Joey Albanese

Jordan Allison

Dawn Anglin

Claude, Nolan, Rem & Tina Bailey

David & Kara Bailey

Leah, Lou, Eliot, Dennis & Philip Bailey

Kim Baker

Maddie Baker

Ellie Balk

Carla Bond Baranowski

Elizabeth & Theresa Baranowski

Keith Bazier

Jonel Beach

Noelle Becker

Dominique Begnaud

Phil, Lydia, Stacia & Theresa Berwick

Ana & Gabe Bonfili

James Bonsanti

Nathan Bookout

Mike Brandon

Alex Braun

Dr. Crystal & April Breeden Peairs

Anthony Brescia

Kim Bromeier

Deneishea Bryant

Janice & Jade Bugett-Hygrade

Joan & Julie Bugnitz

Karen Bult

Mary Beth Bussen

Christina Carroll

Kaleena Casem

Breanna Cashel

Angela Catchings

Lisa & Sophia Chabot

Diedre & Felice Chatman

Sherri Chisholm

Marnie Claunch

Adam Cook

Andy, Linda, Sarah & Emily Cross

Thomas Culler

Fabia D'Amore-Krug

Carly Davis

Damon Davis

Kareem Deanes

Isabella & Sophia DeFord

Veronica Delgado

Allison Dent

Blaine Deutsch & Laura Neuwirth

Kalyn & Julia Neuwirth-Deutsch

Aaron Dickerson

Dahven White & Allen Doctor

Reid, Chase & Moxie Doctor

Sarah, Jack, Taylor & Katie Donato

Kiley Donovan

Dan Duncan

Monica Brendel Duwel

Darcy, Eddie & Val Edwin

Rebecca Eilering

Meredith Elkin

Marcia Ellis

Krista Estes

Lisa, Laila & Parisa Faramarzi

Renee Farmar

Rebecca Fehlig & Family

Eleonore Fischer

Liza Fishbone

LeAnn Fisher

Brian Flynn

Rebecca & Meg Flynn

Lancelot Fordyce III

Elyse & Tyler Frazier

Amber Funicelli

Sarah Carmen Geiss

Karen Gold

Sheri Goldsmith

Shine Goodie

Abby Gordon

Dana Gray

Kurt Greenbaum

Kevin Gregory

Allison Hake

Mikey, Genevieve & Cecilia Halaska

Cheyenne & Quron Harris

Onnie Harrison

Dianne Hartle

Adrienne Hawkins

Mary Belth Heiligenstein

Amanda Helman

Dixie Herrington

Alison Armstrong Hillman

Theresa Hopkins

Tara Howarth

Tracy Hudson

Albert & ZoeyAnn Huff

Jason Hunt

Rita Hunt

Zaire Imani

Meagan Impellizzeri

Emily Davis & Dwayne Isgrig

Isiah, Zeke & Naomi Davis-Isgrig

Carly Jacobs

Loren Jenks

Diana Johnson

Angela Jones

Cory & Drew Keathley

Elizabeth Knight

Rob Knight

Laura Knoblock

Darci & Stasie Knowles

Mary Krummenacher

Josh, Eavan & Ansel Kryah

Jen Kubiszewski
Sir Charles Laplander
Stephanie Larimer
Tom & Kim Litton
Susan Logsdon
Lucia & Sofia Lonero
Charlene Lopez
Jennifer, Mikie, Joey & Gabe Lumetta
Heidi Lung
Tammy Turner Maclean
Annie Martineau
Jordan Massey
Ja'Mel McCaine
Acadia McGee
Andrea McMurray
Kimberly Lorrene Melahn
Carrie Meyer
Kristen Middeke
Magdaline Middeke
Jeff Miller
Joe Mohr

Anne Moore
Katelyn Moore
April, Brenda & May Morrison
Shuka Moshiri
Racquel Mosley
Dawn, Grace, Nate & Stephen Murphy
Robin, Mac, Seda & Daegan Murphy
Merle, Cynthia & Parris Nathan
Marcela Navarrete
Joyce Neikirk
Eric Wolfgang & Brittany Nelson
Emma Nowlin
Darius Overbey
Christine Palmer
Brandon Pappert
Megan Glori Parker
Anastasia Parks

Donald, Amanda, Don Jr. & Demetrius Partee
Libby Pedersen
Laura Pennington
Nelson Perez, Jr.
Ryan Pier
Shannon Piva Piwowarczyk
Frank Popper
Jody Porter
Cheryl Punzalan
Michael & Julie Quintero
Kelley Ray
Isabelle Raymond
Richard & Karen Norman Reilly
Sarah Anne Rennie
Molly Rodgers
Grace Rogers
AJ Rosenberg
Kobi Rowland
Lauren Rundquist

Becky Kern-Ryan
Avi, Ethan & Lissie Ryan
Chris Sabatino
Paul Sager
Lisa Sanditz
Jenn Sarti
Laurel Schmitt
Kristin Serafini
Theodosia & Paisley Sessen
Mary Shay
Alex Sheen
Elizabeth Simons
Jason Skrbec
Abbi Smith
Natalie & Alex Smithey
Maurice St. Pierre
Emily Stafford
Keith Stephens
Jennifer Stiller
Tessa Stoverink
Jon Strauser
Mark Swain
Lisa Tang
George Taylor
Amina Terry
The Thayer Family
Lavette Thomas
Reggie Thomas
Mary Timmel
Anya Toler
Logan Trupiano
Hyanneke van der Pennen
Gary Voss
Jenny Walker

Elizabeth Walters
Christine Warner
Elysia Webber
Moe Weiss
Anna, Maddie & Culeen Wenger
Stephanie Wheat & Christopher Lemeth Wheat
Maggie Wheelock
Meghan Kearney White
Autumn Wiggins
Dale Wilke
David & Peggy Williamson
Amber Withycombe
Peat Wollaeger
Jonny Xacto

The story of *Painting for Peace in Ferguson* would not be possible if it were not for the work of the more than 300 artists, volunteers, church groups and whole families listed here who gave of their time and talent. Despite cold weather and busy holiday schedules, they chose to make a difference in their community in November 2014. As the businesses have made repairs, the plywood boards and the artwork, once so vital to lifting Ferguson's spirits, have come down. This book however, will continue to capture this moment of goodwill and community outreach and the compelling works of art that were the result.

BEFORE

AFTER

From the Artists

"It felt great to be a part of something positive and beautiful that would let people know we haven't given up on the neighborhood. I hope we can come together to find a NEW NORMAL."

Amina – Ferguson artist who painted with her 8-month-old daughter and 83-year-young mother

"We absolutely fell in love with Ferguson and we realized that you don't have to know someone to love them. For us, Ferguson symbolized hope. It was one of the most rewarding things we've done in our lives."

Marcela – Volunteer from Chicago who traveled to Ferguson to participate in Paint for Peace STL

"As a resident of Ferguson, I knew I had to go out and do whatever I could for my neighbors and the businesses. I felt the world had seen us as monsters and thugs, but we are just like you and your community. I believed the paintings would help show the world that we were human, we wanted peace."

Reggie – Ferguson resident

"Working on the mural brought together a broad range of people from all around greater St. Louis. People were having conversations there that they hadn't had before about race and inequality."

Lisa – St. Louis native – New York-based professional fine artist

"While my group was painting a mural, a mother and her young son pulled over and asked if she could take a picture of her son in front of it. As she left, tears of joy rolled down her face as she told the whole group 'thank you.' That brief moment is how I will forever remember the aftermath of Ferguson."

Kelley – Ferguson resident

About the Author

Carol Swartout Klein grew up in Ferguson, and was so inspired by witnessing the spirit of hundreds of volunteers coming together to bring hope to a community in shock that she wanted to capture the story and *Painting for Peace in Ferguson* is the result. A journalist and marketing professional by training Klein always wanted to do a children's book. She saw how the actual process of creating the artwork was healing for all those involved … as the community came together to help others, the artists, business owners and volunteers actually benefitted themselves … and created new connections that she hopes will continue in the future.